Judging the Authenticity of
Early Baseball Cards

\* \* \* \*

David Rudd Cycleback

Judging the Authenticity of Early Baseball Cards
by David Rudd Cycleback
© cycleback 2008, all rights reserved

Publisher: Cycleback.com
ISBN: 978-0-6151-9651-0

**Contents**

1 Introduction
2 Essential tips for total beginning collectors
3 Other resources
4 Special equipment
5 Authenticity
6 How early cards were made, reprinted and identified
7 Identifying reprints by comparison with original cards
8 Embossed cards
9 Gilded cards
10 Black light: an easy way to identify many fakes
11 Using a microscope: introduction
12 Under the microscope: modern printing
13 Under the microscope: 1800s chromolithography
14 Under the microscope: early chalk & crayon lithography
15 Under the microscope: early 1900s color lithography
16 Under the microscope: photoengraving
17 Real photo baseball cards
18 Final note on printing
19 Altered reprints
20 Provenance
21 Quick Tips

# ( 1 )
# Introduction

This guide is about making sound judgments concerning the authenticity, or lack thereof, of pre-1930 baseball cards. This includes identifying reprints, counterfeits, forgeries and fakes. While a small book hardly intends to 'cover it all' or make each reader into an auction house expert, it offers information and techniques that should make anyone a smarter collector. Even learning a few here-and-there techniques will allow the reader to detect more fakes and be more confident about purchases.

    This guide is only a supplement to your personal education, knowledge and experience. This education includes following and reading about the hobby, handling and looking at lots of cards and asking lots of questions of dealers, fellow collectors and experts. There is no replacement for hands on experience. With time the collector will know about common fakes and get a feel for authenticity, age, pricing and rarity. Besides, half the fun of collecting is learning about the material, its history and the hobby.

    Making sound judgments requires intelligence and objectivity. While experts make educated guesses, authentication never involves pre-ordained results or rash opinions.

## ( 2 )
## Essential tips for beginning collectors

Collecting baseball cards is a great hobby for boys and girls of all ages. However, all areas of collecting have fakes, reprints and scams.

The following is a brief but important list of tips. The beginner should read these before jumping into the hobby with open pocketbook.

**1) Start by knowing that there are reprints, counterfeits, fakes and scams out there.** If you start by knowing you should be doing your homework, having healthy skepticism of sellers' grand claims and getting second opinions, you will be infinitely better off than the beginner who assumes everything's authentic and all sellers are honest.

**2) Learn all you can about the hobby and cards.** The more you learn and more experience you have, the better off you are.

**3) Realize that novices in any area of collecting are more likely to overestimate, rather than underestimate, the value of items they own or are about to buy**

**4) Get second opinions and seek advice when needed.** This can range from a formal opinion from a top expert, to input about pricing from a collecting friend. Collectors who seek advice and input are almost always better off than those who are too proud or embarrassed to ask questions.

**5) Find out if a card grader is reputable before you purchase the graded card.** Professional card graders authenticate a card, assign a condition grade (Poor to Mint) and put the card in a labeled holder. Many collectors use graders as an educated independent opinion and to facilitate sales. Many collectors prefer to buy expensive or esoteric cards that have already been graded.

It is important to not assume that all card graders are equal, because they aren't. Some are little more than scams.

Cards than have been graded and authenticated by PSA (Professional Sportscard Authenticators), SGC (Sportscard Guarantee), Beckett (BVG) and GAI (Global Authentication Inc) can be reliably considered to be authentic. Collectors will argue about who is best at grading and identifying alterations, but these graders are reliable at telling the difference between a real and reprint T206, 1933 Goudey or Old Judge. PSA and SGC are currently the most popular with Pre-War collectors.

**6) Start by buying inexpensive items**. Put the 1933 Goudey Babe Ruths, 1952 Mickey Mantles and mint grade T206s off until some other day.

Without exception, all beginners make mistakes. From paying too much to misjudging rarity to buying fakes. It makes sense that a collector should want to make his inevitable beginning mistakes on $10 rather that $1,000 purchases.

**7) Gather a list of good sellers**. A good seller is someone who is knowledgeable and trustworthy. A good seller fixes a legitimate problem when it arises.

Ask other collectors who they like. Discover good sellers on your own by buying a few inexpensive items from an eBay seller and seeing how good are the transactions.

It's best to buy real expensive items online from good sellers, including those you have dealt with or those who otherwise have strong reputations.

## (3)
## Other resources

<u>Standard Catalog of Baseball Cards</u>, Edited by Don Fluckinger (Krause Publications)
<u>Beckett Almanac of Baseball Cards and Collectables</u> (Beckett Publications)
    The collector should own and regularly reference one of the above price guides. These are monster-sized, over 1,000 pages each. Be careful when purchasing, as the publishers also publish highly abridged versions. While the pricing should be taken with a grain of salt, each book checklists and details most standard issues from the 1800s to today. The beginning collector should stick with cards cataloged in these guides. Both guides are available at amazon.com, Barnes and Noble and many major brick and mortar stores.

<u>Vintage Baseball Card Forum</u> :
http://www.network54.com/Forum/153652
    This is a chat board for enthusiasts of Pre-War baseball cards. Many knowledgeable and experienced collectors, dealers and prominent hobby people visit this board. Includes a good list of links to collector's pages, dealers, auction houses, graders, Old Cardboard magazine and more.

<u>Encyclopedia of Baseball Cards</u> by Lew Lipset. Standard history of early cards.

# (4)
# Special Equipment Used in this Guide

**#1) Longwave Black light**
Also known as an ultraviolet light or UV light, a black light is inexpensive, simple to use and great for identifying many reprints and fakes. With a bit of instruction and practice, even the beginner can get good results.

In a dark room black light make things fluoresce (glow) different colors and intensities. The intensity and color of the fluorescence is based on the atomic structure of the material. Even if two cardstocks look the same in normal daylight, they can fluoresce differently under black light. As detailed later in this book, the fluorescence of cards allows collector to identify many reprints and fakes that might go unnoticed in daylight.

Black lights can be bought in many science, hobby and rock shops (certain models are used to identify gems and crystals). Many handheld models can be found in the $10-$20 range on eBay and amazon.com.

<u>It is recommended that the reader buy a longwave instead of a shortwave black light.</u> While shortwave lights are useful in gem and stamp authentication, the longwave is much safer and all you need for trading cards. Most inexpensive examples offered on eBay and amzon.com are longwave. Shortwave is more of a specialty light, more limited on the market and often more expensive. Any black light that is advertised as being useful for black light paint and posters, invisible ink and stamps, identifying restoration and fakes, fluorescent cosmetics and body paint, identifying pet urine and scorpions is most probably the longwave black light you want.

If a black light is listed as being UVA (ultraviolet A), that's the longwave you want. If it's listed as UVB or UVC, that's the shortwave you don't want. Also, the frequency in nanometers (nm) is often listed. If a light is listed as having a frequency of somewhere between 320 and 400nm, it is the longwave you want. Most longwave black lights I've seen for sale were listed in around the 360-395 range. A frequency lower than 315 will be in the more dangerous UVB and UVC range.

It is the responsibility of the reader to learn the safety precautions. For example don't stare directly at the light. Directions that accompany the black light should be read and followed. However, with proper use, longwave black lights are perfectly safe and are even used by kids in elementary school class. Normal sunlight contains longwave black light. While we avoid overexposure to sunlight and wear suntan oil and sunglasses and don't stare directly at the sun, sunlight's nothing to be scared of. In fact, exposure to longwave black light is probably safer than exposure to direct sunlight.

**Tips on effective use of black light**
A black light must be used in a dark room, the darker the better. Take a minute or three to let your eyes get adjusted to the dark. The cards being examined should be on something that does not fluoresce. Something that does not fluoresce will appear black under black light. If your background fluoresces too brightly, it can be hard to judge the fluorescence of the cards.

It's best for the card to be removed from any holder. The holder itself can have a fluorescence or otherwise mask the card's fluoresce. Shine the black light on all sides of the cards. Some cards and photographs have coatings on one side than can change the fluorescence.

For comparison purposes, you may wish to have a shard

of modern paper that fluoresces brightly. Between the black table and bright shard, you will have a range on the spectrum for comparison.

Practice using the black light. See what cards from all years look like under black light. Feel free to look at magazines, books, typing paper, glass, plastic. Antique glass (Tiffany lamp shades, vases, bottles) fluoresce a variety of interesting colors.

### #2 Hand-held Microscope of 50x or more power

As shown in later chapters, microscopic examination of a card's printing is used to judge the age. There are many different and affordable styles. 100x (100 times power) pocket-sized examples can be found on eBay for under $20, and do a credible job. Many have a built in light which is a great convenience. Go to eBay and do a search for *pocket 100x microscope*, or similar wording, and a few will likely pop up. Amazon.com likely has some for sale as well.

## (5)
## Authenticity

In all areas of collecting, from teddy bears to oil paintings, something is authentic if its true identity is described accurately and sincerely.

If you pay good money for an "original 1930 Greta Garbo photograph by the famous Hollywood photographer George Hurrell" you expect to receive an original 1930 Greta Garbo photo by George Hurrell. You don't expect a 1970 reprint or a photo by an unknown photographer.

An item does not have to be rare or expensive or old to be authentic. It just has to be accurately and sincerely described. A 2 cent 2003 reprint can be authentic if described as a 2 cent 2003 reprint.

Errors in the description of an item are considered significant when they significantly affect the financial value or reasonable non-financial expectations of the buyer. An example of the reasonable non-financial expectations would involve a collector who specializes in real photo post cards of her home state of Iowa and makes it clear to the seller that she only wants postcards depicting Iowa. Even if there is no financial issue, she would have reason to be disappointed if the purchased postcard turned out to show Oklahoma or Minnesota.

Many errors in description are minor and have little to no material effect. If that 1930 Greta Garbo photo turns out to be from 1934, it may not effect the financial value or desirability to the purchaser.

**Common terms:**
**Counterfeit**: a reprint or reproduction that was intentionally made to fool others into believing it is original.

**Forgery**: an item that was intentionally made to fool others into believing it is something it is not. This includes counterfeits, but also fantasy or made up items. An example of a fantasy would be a 1958 Bowman Mickey Mantle. Bowman did not make baseball cards after 1955, so a 1958 Bowman Mantle never existed.

**Fake**: an item that is seriously misidentified. This includes forgeries and counterfeits. It also includes items that are innocently misidentified by collectors or sellers who are uninformed.

When in doubt about seller or maker's intent, it's best to call a bad sale or auction item a fake instead of a forgery or counterfeit. All three words mean an item is not genuine, but forgery and counterfeit implies intentional illegality.

**It's about making judgments**
This guide isn't about becoming omniscient or gaining supernatural authentication powers. It's about forming sound opinions based on your knowledge, experience, tools, resources and common sense.

With many cards you will be confident to certain they are genuine.

With many cards you will be confident to certain they are fakes or otherwise have significant errors in description.

A percentage of cards you won't be able to make a definitive opinion. Perhaps the card is outside your area of collecting. Perhaps the card has something strange about it, but not strange enough to prove it fake. Perhaps you strongly believe the unusual card is old, but aren't sure what it is or the exact year of issue as it isn't listed in the price guides.

There's nothing wrong with being stumped every once

in a while. Even the top experts at Mastro and SGC will sometimes scratch their heads and seek outside opinions.

**Judging authenticity is rarely done in a vacuum**
For the collector, making judgments is usually done within a context. Usually the context is deciding whether or not to purchase and how much to pay.

A knowledgeable collector might take a wild chance on a strange card if the price is $30, while she would pass if the price was $500. A collector might purchase an esoteric card if he knows the seller to be knowledgeable, but wouldn't give it a second glance if the seller had a reputation for selling fakes.

You never have to buy a card or piece of memorabilia. If you are uncomfortable with the looks of a card, the price or the reliability of the seller, you can choose not to bid or buy.

## (6)
## How early cards were made, reprinted and are identified: A quick overview

This chapter offers a quick background for the rest of the book.

**How 1800s Cards Were Made**

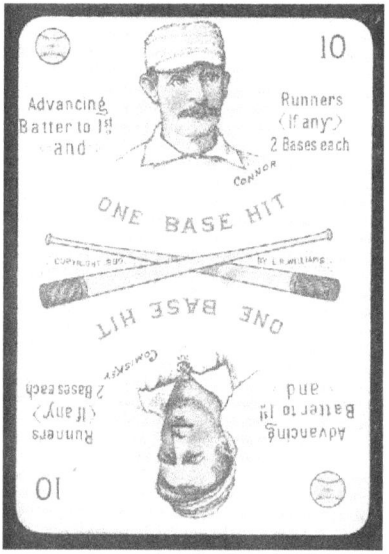

1889 E.R. Williams Game Card

Most 1800s baseball cards were made using antiquated methods.

Many 1800s cards have actual photographs pasted to cardboard backing. This includes the Old Judges, Gypsy Queens, Lone Jacks and all those other cards with sepia photorealistic images.

Those colorful 1880s Allen & Ginters, Buchner Gold

Coin, Goodwin Champions, cartoon trade cards and similar were 'handmade' lithographs. Handmade means the designs were made directly onto the printing plate by an artist using special hand held tools. There were no modern photomechanical reproduction techniques available to the printers of these cards. When you look at an Allen & Ginter or Tobin Lithograph, it looks like a little color sketch or painting. These cards were made in the same old school way as Picasso and Marc Chagall made their lithographs that hang in museums.

## Halftone Printing and the Introduction of Realistic Printed Images

Though we take for granted the photorealistic pictures printed on Topps cards, magazine covers, cereal boxes and music CD booklets, the technology used to mechanically print realistic pictures did not exist for most of the 1800s.

While the photograph itself has been around since 1839, it took decades before printers could print realistic reproductions of photographs. If you look at an 1860s Harper's Weekly or similar magazine you will see that the pictures resemble hand drawn sketches not photos.

The invention of the *half-tone* printing process allowed for magazines, newspapers and trading cards to have printed photorealistic images. In a complicated processes involving expensive printing machinery, halftone uses a special screen to translate a photographic image into a pattern of fine dots on the printing plate and the resulting print. This fine dot pattern allowed for detail that could not be achieved before.

If you take a good magnifying glass and examine a modern magazine picture or baseball card, you will see this dot pattern. For a black and white picture, the dots are only black. For a color picture, the dots will be various colors.

For baseball cards, the halftone printing was used only on part of the card. In the following 1963 Topps card, the player's picture, including uniform, hands and face, is made up of the halftone dots. The border design and text are solid ink.

### The history of half-tone printing on baseball cards
All or close to all of today's baseball cards are made with halftone printing. A large portion of the early 1900s cards were made with halftone. If you check out a 1920s Exhibit or 1915 Sporting News you will see the dots. However, only a few 1800s baseball cards were made with halftone printing. This includes the 1890s Just So Tobacco and N300 Mayo Cut Plug and one or two obscure and rare trade cards.

**Other types of early 1900s cards**
Many early 1900s cards were color lithographs. This includes the T206s, T205s, T3 Turkey Reds and many caramel cards. Though made with more a slightly more advanced technology than in the 1800s, these issues carry on the colorful, artistic tradition of the Allen & Ginters.

A few early 1900s cards were actual photographs like in the 1800s. These include the T200 and T222 Fatimas, Fatima Premiums and T5 Pinkerton Cabinets.

**How reprints and counterfeits are made**
Modern cards are made with modern cardstock and modern printing techniques. Many cheap reprints are made with home computer printers, which obviously weren't around before World War II.

I've never seen or heard of a modern reprint or counterfeit of a baseball card made with the original technology.

**How reprints and counterfeits are identified**
Reprints and counterfeits are identified in a variety of ways. They almost always are significantly different in one or more ways than an original.

Many reprints and counterfeits don't closely resemble the original, perhaps being of wrong size, coloring or just looking bad. An active collector of T206s and T205s will often be able to identify a reprint of those issues upon first look. Many reprints are identified when compared to known genuine cards.

Many cards are commonly known as fakes and in person examination is not needed. It is widely known that original Fro Joy Babe Ruth cards were only black and white, and all color versions are reprints.

As this guide shows, there are techniques a collector can use to identify a reprint of an issue he doesn't specialize in.

The black light can identify cardstock that is modern. Even if not a printing expert, collectors can learn to identify modern printing.

**How cards are authenticated**
Authentication and forgery detection are related but not the same thing. You could say authentication is forgery detection at a deeper level.

If a 1933 Goudey Babe Ruth says "reprint" on the back, you don't have to be an expert to identify it as a reprint. However, if the 1933 Goudey Ruth card does not say "reprint" on back, does that mean it's original? Of course not. Many Goudey fakes have no reprint designation on back.

We've all said at one time or other about a card or piece of memorabilia, "I don't see anything wrong, but I wish there is some way I could be certain it was genuine."

Along with hands on experience and general knowledge of cards and the input of hobby friends, the expert uses a variety of techniques to authenticate cards. Some techniques are simple, like comparing a card to another from the issue. Some techniques, like print identification and dating, are so advanced that an expert can date a baseball card he has never even seen before.

# ( 7 )
## Identifying counterfeits and reprints by comparing with genuine cards

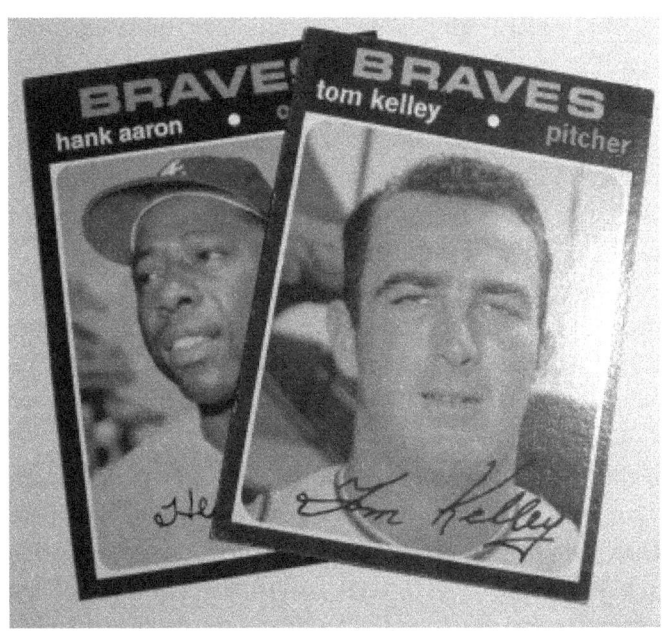

A standard and often highly effective way to detect counterfeits and reprints is by directly comparing the card in question with one or more known genuine examples.

Granted, it is uncommon for the collector to already own duplicates, especially if it's a 1933 Goudey Babe Ruth or 1965 Topps Joe Namath. However, good judgment is often made when comparing a card to different cards from the same issue. Comparing the Ruth to a bunch of Goudey commons and the Namath to a handful of other 1965 Topps.

A T206 Ty Cobb, and even a T206 Honus Wagner, was printed on the same sheet as T206 commons. The printers did not bring out special cardstock and VIP inks for the superstars. When you are studying the qualities of T206 commons, you are also studying the qualities of the T206 Honus Wagner and Ed Plank.

If there are cards insufficient in number or of extra poor quality (caught in the back yard thresher), techniques discussed later in this guide will be essential.

In nearly all cases, counterfeits and reprints are significantly different than the real card in one and usually more than one way. However, in many cases, even though a difference or two is identified (cardboard a bit thinner and lighter in color), this doesn't answer whether the difference is due to fakery or is a genuine variation. Techniques from later in this guide will be needed.

Comparing cards is highly effective in identifying modern counterfeits. If you know how to properly compare cards, you should be able to identify a fake 1986-7 Fleer Michael Jordan and 1979-80 OPC Wayne Gretzky.

Before examination, the collector should be aware of variations within an issue. A genuine 1956 Topps baseball card can be found on dark grey or light grey cardboard. While the 1887 Old Judges are usually sepia in color, pink examples can be found. The examiner must also take into consideration reasonable variations due to aging and wear. A stained card may be darker than others. An extremely worn or trimmed card may be shorter and lighter in weight than others in the issue. A card that has glue on back will allow less light through when put up to the light. The collector will often have to make a judgment call when taking these variations into effect. This is why having experience with a variety of cards is important.

The following is a short list of things to look at. You are welcome to add your own things to the list.

**Obvious Differences**: This can include text or copyright date indicating the card is a reprint, major size difference, wrong back. Many of these problems are obvious even in an online scan.

If you are experienced with an issue, perhaps you've collected Goudeys for the last few years, most reprints and counterfeits within that issue will obvious. They simply will look bad.

**Dimensions of face and back**: This can do be done through comparison with numerous other cards. Price guides will list the size for standard issues.

**Dimensions of printing**: This includes size of the image, borders and text. Most counterfeits made by photocopiers will have correct measurements. However, a counterfeit of the 1956 Topps Willie Mays card had the correct card measurement but the print itself, including the image of Mays, was too large. This created borders around the image that were too thin.

**Solid areas**: With a magnifier or microscope, compare which areas are solid and which are not. On a genuine T206, the border around the player picture and the player's name and team below is solid. While many reprints will also have these areas solid, many will not.

On the 1971 Topps cards, the faux signatures in the front player picture is solid black. On many reprints the faux signature will be made up of a dot pattern.

The reprint 1971 Topps on the right has a different tone cardstock and is much glossier than the genuine card on the left. In person, difference is obvious.

**Appearance of card stock and surfaces**: This includes color, texture, feel, etc. The correct gloss is hard to duplicate on a reprint, and most reprints will have different gloss than the original. Make sure to check both sides. T206s and 1951 Bowmans, for examples, have different textures front versus back. Make sure to check the thickness, color and appearance of the card's thickness or edge. The edge often shows the cardstock to be different, especially when the counterfeiter has pasted a computer paper reprint onto cardstock. Obviously different cardstock is one of the most common giveaways of reprints and counterfeits.

**Font and size of lettering and border lines**: Some reprinters go to the effort of recreating the lettering and border lines, making them solid like with the originals. In many of these reprints, the font of the lettering is noticeably off. This includes the thinness of the lines, height of the letters, and the distance between lines of lettering. If you are familiar with an issue, the lettering on one of these reprints will be strikingly different on first glace. Similarly, the border lines and designs may be noticeably different. Many T206 reprints have a distinctly different font to the name plate below the image.

**Unnatural signs of reproduction:** In some cases, thoughtless errors appear on a forgery that has been photocopied or computer scanned. If a piece of lint or dirt was on the photocopier or scanner, it may appear on the reprint. A photocopier forgery of the 1952 Bowman card of Mickey Mantle has a small white mark on his chin that doesn't appear on genuine cards.

The genuine card used for reproduction may have a crease or scrape which can literally felt on the genuine card, but is only reproduced on the reprint.

This computer reprint of a 'Safe Hit' food packaging label has a picture-only of the folding creases. If it were real, you would be able to feel the crease lines with your finger and see the bend with your eyes. Pictures-only of creases, scrapes and dirt sometimes appear in reprints, especially home made computer reprints.

**Opacity**: Opacity is measured by the amount of light that shines through an item, or the 'see through' effect.

Cardstock varies in opacity. Some allow much light through, some allow none, while there rest fall somewhere in between. Most dark cardboard let through little if any light. White stocks usually let through more. While two cardboard samples may look identical in color, texture and thickness, they may have different opacity. This could be because they were made they were made in different plants, at a different time and/or were made from different substances.

Testing opacity is a good way to compare card stock. The same cards should have the same or similar opacity. Many reprints will have distinctly different opacity than the real cards.

Opacity tests should be done with more than one card from the issue. Comparisons should take into consideration variations due to age, staining, soiling and other wear, along with known card stock variations in the issue. It must be taken into consideration that normal differences in ink on the card will affect opacity. If one genuine T206 card has a darker picture (a dark uniformed player against dark background), it should let less light through than a genuine T206 card with a lighter picture (a white uniformed player against a light sky).

The opacity test can detect many restored expensive cards. In the past, some genuine but low grade star cards (1933 Goudey Ruth, T206 Cobb) have been restored in part by having the rounded corners rebuilt with paper fibers from other cards and glue. When held to the light, the built up corners are often seen as they let through a different amount of light than the rest of the card. These restored cards are high end cards that have mint or close to mint appearance. It's not something done to a 1976 Topps common.

The reprinted 1971 Topps (left) lets through much more light than the original 1971 Topps on the right. This helps show the cards are made out of significantly different card stock.

**Black Light Test**
Studying the degree and color of fluorescence under a black light is an unbeatable tool for comparing ink and cardboard. If you spread out in the dark a pile of 1983 Topps with the exception that one is a 1983 OPC, the OPC will be easy to pick out with black light. The OPC is made out of a different card stock and fluoresces many times brighter than the Topps stock.

This is the way it often works for reprints and counterfeits. Reprints and counterfeits were made with different cardstock and often fluoresce differently than the genuine cards. The reprint may fluoresce darker, lighter or with a different color. In some cases a reprint and an original may fluoresce the same, but in many cases the black light will help you pick out reprints with ease.

* * * *

Often, the differences between a questioned card and genuine examples will be significant enough that the collector will be nearly certain it is a fake. Remember that in most cases a reprint will be different than the real cards in multiple ways, usually multiple major ways. If that 1984 Topps Dan Marino rookie has a significantly different gloss, thickness, fluorescence, cardstock color and opacity from genuine 1984 Topps commons, the card is more than probably a reprint. If a T206 has significantly different opacity, gloss and black light fluorescence than your other T206s, it's safe to assume it's not an original T206.

In other cases, the differences will not be significant enough and further tests will be necessary. If the questioned card has a slightly off color, it will take tests described later in this book to determine if the color is due to reproduction or a natural variation on a genuine card.

Even if the differences are significant and obvious, further tests are still warranted to provide definitive proof that it is a fake. For example, the proof of fakery would be irrefutable if black light or microscopic tests show that the cardstock was made recently. If you are having a dispute with a seller who sold you a counterfeit, it is great to be able to say things like "Longwave black light tests show that the cardstock was made Post World War II."

# ( 8 )
# Embossed cards

T204 Ramlys have embossments that can be seen and felt on back and front. No known reprints have this embossment.

A few early baseball card issues are embossed. This includes the T204 Ramlys and R & S Artistic Die Cuts. Few if any reprints or counterfeits of these cards will be embossed. If you think about it, why would a counterfeiter spend the time and effort to fake embossment when there are so many flat cards to reprint? The R & S also have shiny fronts.

While embossment is not in and of itself proof of authenticity, it is strong evidence. If you receive in the mail from an honest seller your first R & S and it is shiny and embossed, you can be confident it is genuine.

# ( 9 )
# Gilded cards

T206 with copper gilded border

A few early baseball cards are gilded. This includes the T205 Gold Borders, T204 Ramlys, Old Judge Cabinets and a number of other sports and non-sport cards.

Gilding is the craft of adding gold or other metal, in the form of leaf or dust, to the surface of materials including metal, glass, wood and paper. 'Gild' literally means gold. Traditionally gold was used, but silver, aluminum, copper, bronze and other metals have been used in recent times.

This non-printing practice is thousands of years old. Ancient Egyptian artifacts and early European religious manuscripts were gilded in real gold. Archeologists date the process to more than 2000 years before Jesus Christ. It was not until the 20th century, after the T205 were made, that an effective method of printing in metal was developed.

While there are numerous methods and variations in gilding that result in a variety of appearances, the practice used on old trading cards was as follows. The gold or silver colored metal was in the form of dust or flakes. On the card a glue, called sizing, was applied in the desired pattern. After a short wait, but before the sizing was dried, the metal flakes was applied. The metal dried in place, creating the desired metallic finish.

This means that the T205, T204 Ramlys and other gilded cards have areas that are literally covered in metal dust. Though often tarnished by age, the borders will shine like metal in the correct angle of light.

Before you fire up your backyard smelter, know that the 'gold' borders on most baseball cards are copper not gold.

Modern cards with metal are not gilded, but printed using modern technology. On that insert of Derek Jeter or Brett Favre, the metal is typically stamped in.

Home computer reprints of gilded cards will have printed reproductions of the metal. If you look at the 'gilding' you will see the tell tale multi-color dot ink pattern. Upon close inspection, the printed pattern won't have the quality and shine of real metal. The 'metal' area will have the same or similar gloss as the rest of the card, and you won't be able to feel the metal with your finger.

**Seeing the difference**
The difference between today's metal printed cards and the early cards gilded with metal dust can be seen both with the naked eye and under the microscope.

The metal printing used on most of today's cards is bright and shiny, with no tarnishing. The flat areas are usually completely smooth, like chrome. It often has embossment that can be felt with the finger and seen. This embossment can include lettering, border-line, logo or textured pattern. The embossment will look professional and rigid, like it was stamped by a machine (which it was).

On the old cards, the metal dust is typically tarnished. The surface is flat and can't have the intricate embossment of modern cards. While there may be some cases where the gild is added on top of an already embossed area (which will have a reverse embossment that can be seen and felt on the back of the card), the gilt itself cannot be embossed. The T204 Ramlys are examples of gilding onto an already embossed card.

The vintage gild is delicate and prone to flaking, metal loss and other damage. The gild on the borders make the T205 cards amongst the most condition sensitive of all baseball cards. The gild is often partially or totally missing on the edges of the Old Judge Cabinets, as it flaked off with time and handling. When looking at the gild in an angle of light that makes it shine, it has the appearance of dust—an uneven, dust-like appearance.

The areas to be gilded on the small tobacco cards were often first printed in yellow. This was to enhance the gold, and make any scratches or flaking less noticeable. You will occasionally see T205s without the metal and the borders are yellow. It will often be yellow where metal has flaked off.

**Under the microscope**
If you have a microscope you will really see the difference between gilding and modern printed cards. On a T205 you will often be able see the individual specks of metal and the yellow ink beneath. It will look like a miniature gold mine. The metal on a modern card, on the other hand, looks like a gold bar— completely solid often with mechanical patterns of embossment.

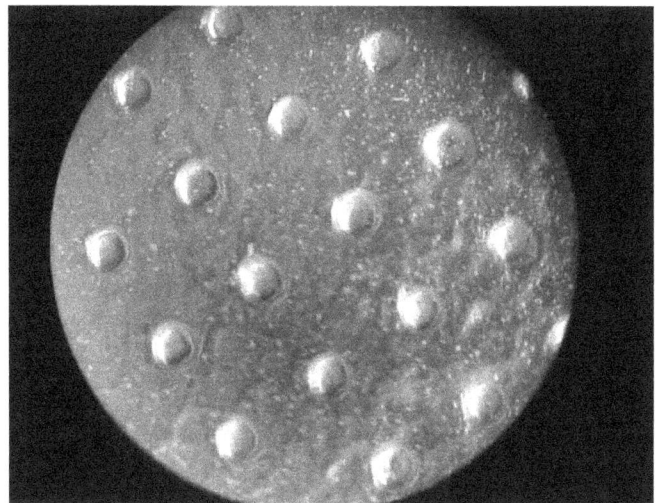

**1990s baseball card shown at 100X Magnification.** The metal is solid and with an embossed pattern. Looks like a bar of gold.

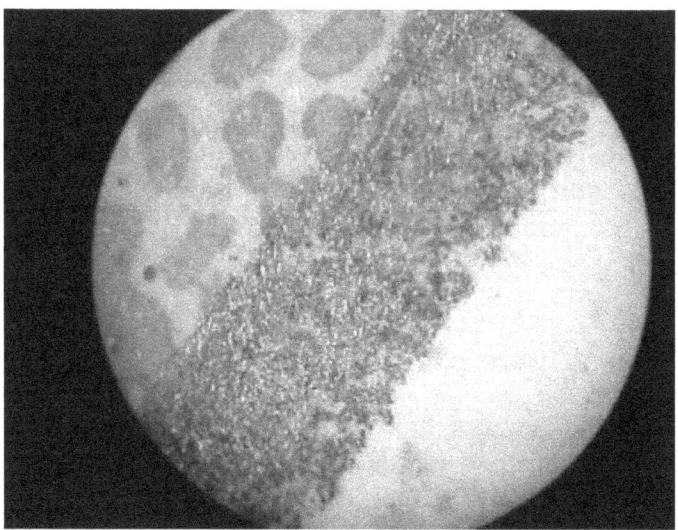

**Vintage gilding.** Microscopic view (100X Power) of the gilding on a turn of the century card, with the flakes of tarnished metal.

**Gilding as a sign of authenticity**
Gilding, in its wide variety of forms and appearances, is still practiced in the arts and crafts. I saw a modern book on refinishing and restoring furniture that has a chapter on how to gild table legs and the like. My retired painter neighbor occasionally gilds his paintings and their frames.

In a practical sense, it is unlikely that a counterfeiter of a T205 baseball card is going to gild it with metal dust. Unlike printing a T206 Honus Wagner off a home computer, gilding is a craft performed by professionals or experienced amateurs. The necessary time, skill and expense is prohibitive to the counterfeiter. Even if the counterfeiter was to actually gild the T205 reprint, it would be nearing impossible to give it the same tone, sheen, color and tarnish of real T205 gild. Besides if you add gild to a crappy reprint, it will still look like a crappy reprint.

While genuine gild on a vintage card does not in and of itself authenticate, the presence is significant evidence of authenticity. If your T205s have tarnished gild on the borders, you probably own authentic T205s. If you find a Jack Johnson boxing card you have not seen before and it has genuine gilding on the borders or back, you will know the metal was added by an old time process and the average reprint or counterfeit wouldn't have it.

## ( 10 )
## Black light : an easy way to identify many reprints and fakes

A longwave black light is great tool for quickly identifying reprints and fakes of Pre World War II paper material. This includes baseball cards, but also photographs, programs, posters, postcards, tickets and anything made of paper.

**Identification of Modern Papers Using Black Light**
A black light is effective in identifying many, though not all, modern paper stocks.

    Starting in the late 1940s, manufacturers of many products began adding *optical brighteners* and other new chemicals to their products. Optical brighteners are invisible dyes that fluoresce brightly under ultraviolet light. They were used to make products appear brighter in normal daylight, which contains some ultraviolet light. Optical brighteners were added to laundry detergent and clothes to help drown out stains and to give the often advertised 'whiter than white whites.' Optical brighteners were added to plastic toys to makes them brighter and more colorful. Paper manufacturers joined the act as well, adding optical brighteners to many, though not all of their white papers stocks.

    A black light can identify many trading cards, posters, photos and other paper items that contain optical brighteners. In a dark room and under black light optical brighteners will usually fluoresce a very bright light blue or bright white. To find out what this looks like shine a recently made white trading card, snapshot or most types of today's printing paper under a black light.

If paper stock fluoresces very bright as just described, it almost certainly was made after the mid 1940s.

It is important to note that not all modern papers will fluoresce this way as optical brighteners are not added to all modern paper. For example, many modern wirephotos have no optical brighteners. This means that if a paper doesn't fluoresce brightly this does not mean it is necessarily old. However, with few exceptions, if a paper object fluoresces very brightly, it could not have been made before World War II. I put my modern paper photo collection under longwave black light, and over 80 percent of the paper fluoresced brightly.

It is important that the collector gain practical experience. This means using a black light to examine and compare the fluorescence of a variety of items. With photographs, make sure you shine the black light on all sides and edges. This is because the gelatin or other coating on the front of the paper often prevents the front from fluorescing.

The beauty of this black light test is you can use it on items you aren't an expert on. You may be no expert on 1920s German Expressionist movie posters or 1890s Italian opera programs, but you can still identify many modern reprints.

## ( 11 )
## Using a Microscope : Introduction

One of the best aids for authentication is the pocket microscope of 50x-100x power. With experience and the knowledge of what things look like, the collector can make good judgments about the age of baseball card printing. Being able to correctly judge the age of printing on a baseball card is a rare and invaluable skill.

Printing is as much a technology as computers, televisions and medicine. As with all technologies, printing has changed over the years. The printing used to make a 1910 card is different than used to make a 1990 card. Under the microscope, the differences are visible. The expert can look at a card at the microscopic level and determine if the printing is old or new.

A knowledgeable collector can look at a 1916 Sporting News Jim Thorpe and say, "This is period printing. This card is genuine." Or she can look at a T206 Eddie Plank and say, "The multi-color dot pattern in the image proves that this card is a modern reprint."

The power of this type of printing examination is that the collector can make sound judgments about a card he has never before seen in person. If you have not seen a 1913 National Game card before, you can look at one under the microscope and be certain it is vintage.

Even if you don't wish to become a printing expert, you can learn a few simple rules that will help you identify many reprints. Just read the next chapter.

The following chapters will look at the most common forms of printing used to make early cards, along with the reprints and forgeries. The pictures shown are snapshots from a given card at a given spot. What you see on cards will often vary in colors and form. For example, T206 with a red uniformed player will have more red than a T206 with a blue uniformed player. Looking at a variety of cards on your own is important.

## (12)
## To know what is old, you must know what is new

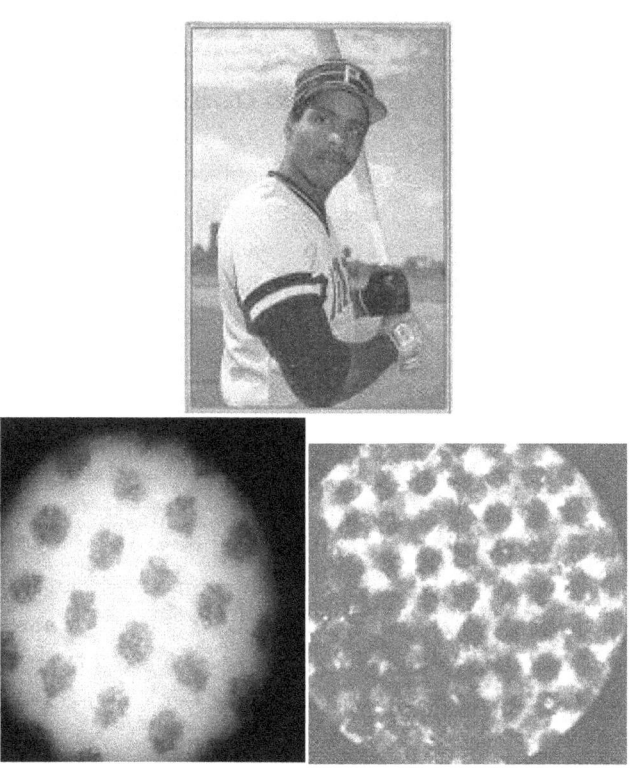

**1987 Barry Bonds**

In this chapter you will learn what the printing on early baseball cards does not look like.

While lithography itself has been around for over two hundred years, the version used to make modern trading cards, including reprints and counterfeits, is easy to identify.

If you examine the color player picture on the front of a modern trading card, like that Barry Bonds, you will see the image is made up of a fine pattern of tiny color dots (the card's text, border lines and other designs will often be solid ink). This is color half-tone printing, and it is used to make the pictures for many modern products, including magazines, books, postcards and cereal boxes. You can examine any of those and other commercial products and see the dots pattern.

The combination of color dots creates the image and its naked eye color. The individual dots on modern cards are usually yellow, cyan (light blue), magenta (dark pink) and black. They will overlap each other in areas to create the various colors. For example, a yellow dot overlapping a magenta dot will create orange on the microscopic level. As you look in different parts of the image the dot colors and density will change. For a blue sky there will be mostly or totally blue dots. In a light area, there will be few and sometimes no dots. In a dark area there will be lots of different colored dots crowded together, many overlapping. But you will find that the entire image is made up of a mechanical pattern of tiny multi color dots.

If you look at a half tone lithographed dot at high magnification, it will appear like a little splotch of paint or colored glue. The edges will be soft and often splotchy.

Home computer printers and color photocopiers create the same multi color dot pattern, though under high magnification the little dots of ink may not look like splotches of paint.

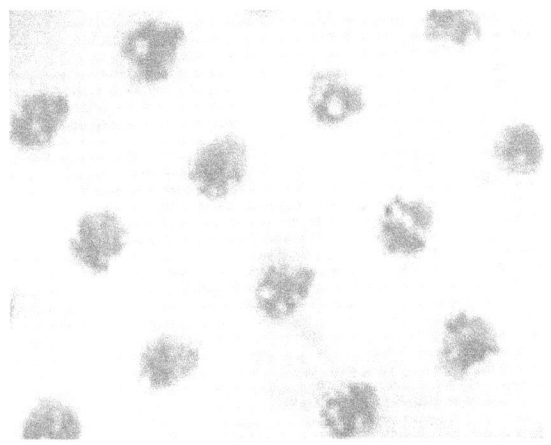
Splotchy, soft edged lithograph dots

## Guess What? You've Just Learn How to Identify Many Reprints

Few if any Pre-1930 baseball cards have images with this type of multi color halftone dots printing pattern. While, as you will see later, black and white halftone was used on some early cards, the multi-color dot pattern was not.

In other words, if you see a T206 Ty Cobb where Cobb's picture has this type of halftone multi dot printing throughout his image, it's a reprint. If you see an Old Judge Hoss Radbourne with this type of printing, its a reprint. If you see an Allen & Ginter Cap Anson with this type of printing, it's a reprint. If you see a Just So Tobacco with the multi-color dot pattern, it's a reprint. If you see a Four Base Hits with this type of printing, it's a reprint. And so on.

Between this chapter and chapter 10 (black light), you can identify more reprints than you can shake a stick at.

## (13)
## 1800s baseball cards lithography:
## "chromolithography"

**Allen & Ginter tobacco cards**

This chapter looks at an early form of lithography used to make many popular 1800s color baseball cards. This type of printing is commonly referred to as chromolithography. Chromolithograph is simply a nickname coined to describe particularly colorful lithography.

The 1800s was before the half-tone dots revolutionized lithography. In those early days, the card images were based on the artist's drawing skill. Many 1800s cards, like the Allen & Ginters, resemble little paintings.
    Under the microscope, the printing looks nothing like the halftone printing of a modern card. Under the microscope, the Allen & Ginter player image looks as if the image was painted in watercolor paint by a tiny brush. The ink marks look like brush strokes sometimes with irregular dots. This is a long way from the rigid pattern of modern half-tone printing.
    The ink is thin and watery, like watercolor paint, and often has an irregular, dark rim around the edge. This is from how the ink settled. This rim effect is typical of early chromolithography and doesn't appear in modern or other types of lithography. This rim often appears in the lettering and border lines on the card.
    As described in a later chapter, a different printing, called photoengraving, also produced a dark edge or rim to the ink. The photoengraving rim is much more rigid and mechanical appearing. Luckily, photoengraving also is an old time printing method. Meaning, whichever the printing method, a microscopic dark rim around the ink helps show the card is old.
    If all this sounds too technical, I recommend you take a microscope and look at Allen & Ginters and T206s yourself. You will see that the printing simply looks nothing like the 1990 Topps card or color magazine picture.

Artists and printers often added dots for shading and toning. This was called 'stippling.' It was added to the printing plate by hand or by a hand held roller with points. Stippling was especially popular in the late 1800s and a large percentage of cards will have it. While stippling somewhat resembles the modern half-tone dots, it can be distinguished. While the half-tone dots would saturate the entire image, stippling was added as an afterthought and usually only in one color. It usually didn't encompass the whole image, but instead was added as shading here and there. Under the microscope the stipple dots are irregularly shaped and sized and have the typical rim at the edges of the ink.

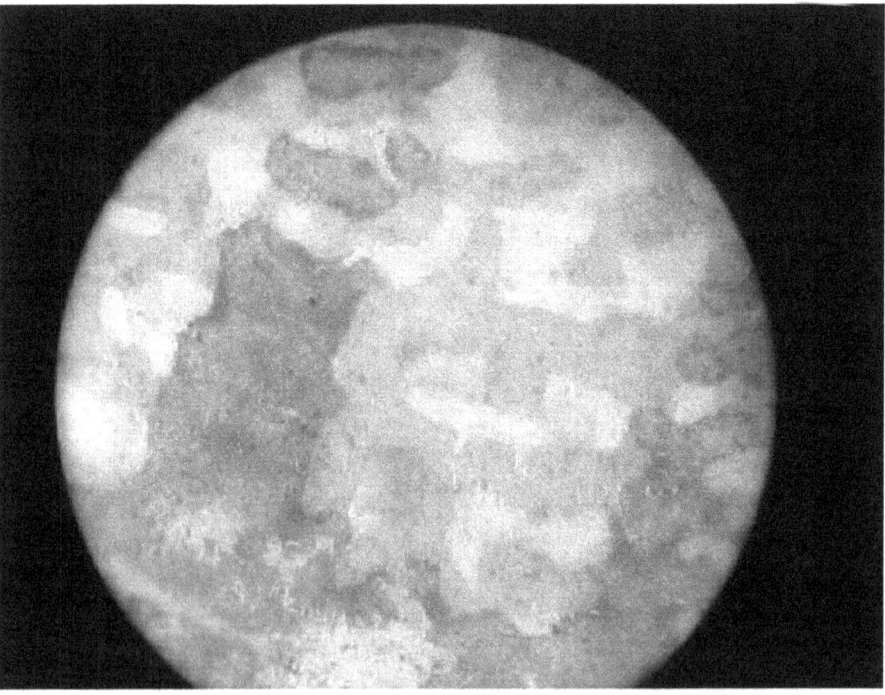

Chromolithography on an 1892 Trade card at 100X power. The ink is watery and messy, like a watercolor painting. No confusing this for a modern halftone print.

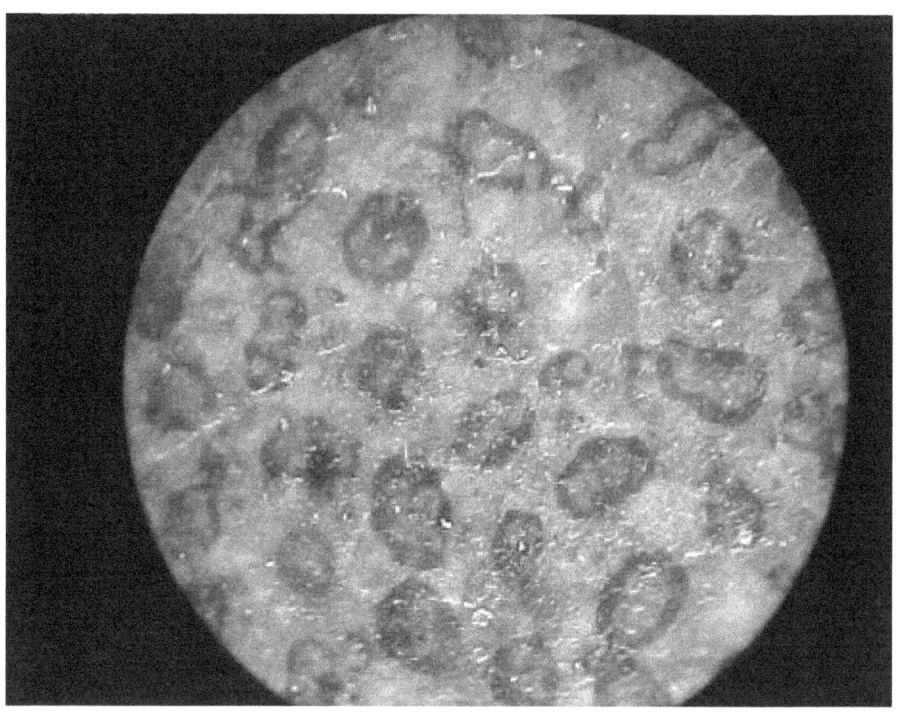

Stipple on a Victorian trade card (100X power). The dots are irregular in shape and size and have the common dark rim around the edges

## ( 14 )
## Another old time printing method: Chalk and crayon lithography

**1800s crayon and chalk lithograph trade card.**

Though not common, the collector will sometimes find 1800s baseball cards, usually trade cards, with chalk and crayon lithography. This type of printing was also used on some early advertising signs, vintage movie posters and fine art prints.

In the fine arts, artists use handmade lithographic techniques to produce a variety of effects. Lithography can create original prints that mimic a pen and ink drawing, a watercolor painting, an etching and a chalk and crayon sketch. Often times, artists mix and match these and other techniques in a single print.

Chalk and crayon lithographs are easily identifiable, because they look like chalk or crayon sketches. A chalk lithograph looks like a chalk sketch and a crayon lithograph looks like a crayon sketch. It's sometimes difficult to tell whether a chalk and crayon lithograph is a print or an actual sketch. Even when viewed up close and under a magnifying glass, the printing will have the subtle detail of an original sketch. There will be no halftone dot pattern.

These lithographs were made by the artist using special lithographic chalk or crayons to draw directly onto the printing plate. This is why the prints so closely resemble original sketches.

One of the great things about chalk and crayon lithography is that it is extremely difficult to counterfeit or reprint deceptively. The printing is simply too tonally subtle and detailed to reproduce so as to fool someone familiar with the printing technique. The only way to reproduce a chalk or crayon lithograph so that it looks halfway decent is to use the modern halftone printing methods. This means that virtually all reproductions of chalk and crayon lithograph cards or posters or signs will have the tell tale halftone dot pattern.

If you have a known trade card, antique sign or advertising poster that resembles a chalk and crayon sketch, even under a loupe or magnifying class, it's likely genuine.

## ( 15 )
## Early 1900s trading card lithography

Early 1900s color lithograph baseball cards, like the T206s, T205s and E101s, used a more advanced form of printing than in the 1800s. However, the lithography was still old fashioned and the player pictures still often resemble little paintings or color sketches.

Again, beyond the printing technicalities, the lithographic printing on these cards simply do not resemble modern half tone printing under the microscope. If you take your microscope and compare the player picture on a T206 and a modern card you will see the drastic difference.

The half-tone process proved popular with photoengraving printing (see next chapter), with photo-realistic black and white images appearing regularly in early 1900s newspapers, magazines and those black and white cards. However, it took much longer for the half-tone process to catch on with color lithography. This was partially due to the early lithographic ink. The ink used for lithography was thinner and unstable, which was not conducive to creating the rigid dot structure necessary for a detailed half-tone print.

Many early 1900s color lithograph cards used the half-tone process, but in a limited and primitive way. Under the microscope a T206 or E95 looks much like the printing on an Allen & Ginter and nothing like a Topps. There may be some areas of dots, but there is no rigid pattern or shape. In some areas the dots may be rigid, but in others they're irregular and strange shaped.

With the T206 Harry Pattee closeup on the cover of this book, you can see how there were black half tone dots in some areas and solid ink in others. There are some black dots on Pattee himself, his face, portions of his hands and uniform. However, the grass, top of the sky, Pattee's hair, top of his cap and the background purple trees have no dots. The halftone dots are only in black ink and only used on a small portion of the image. The rest is solid color ink. On a modern reprint, the whole image would be saturated with tell tale multi-color dots. (Obviously, the cover is a reprinted detail of a T206, and if you examine the book cover with a microscope you will see the fine multi color dot pattern.)

As with the 1800s chromolithography, the ink on the early 1900s color lithograph cards is thin and looks like watercolor under the microscope. The ink often has the distinct irregular dark rim around the edge of the ink. This typical irregular dark rim will also appear on much of the black borders and text below the player's picture. As the back of the card usually has a rough texture, there is usually no detectable rim there. It's best to examine the printing on the smooth front.

**Off registration as a sign of authenticity**
A common problem in the printing of early 1900s color lithograph cards was color registration. Each color was printed with its own printing plate, and the printers had a tough time lining up the colors during the printing process. It is not uncommon for a T206 card to have the colors at the border or edge of the player's body or head to overlap. Sometimes the overlapping is drastic, obvious in an online picture.

You can see slight color overlapping and underlapping on the T206 Harry Pattee on the cover of this book. On the edge of his right arm you can see some blue, which was supposed to be part of the green grass (blue ink + yellow ink = green). On the bottom of the same arm you can see yellow where the blue is missing. On the side of his right arm, you can see a bit of yellow where the blue didn't light up correctly. This off registration is relatively minor. It is often more obvious.

If overlapping color ink is solid, that's a strong sign that your card is genuine. In a cheap home computer reprint, where someone prints out a digital scan of card, it will have a half-tone reproduction of the registration. From afar it may appear like genuine overlapping colors. However, upon close examination you will see the tell tale multi-color dot pattern.

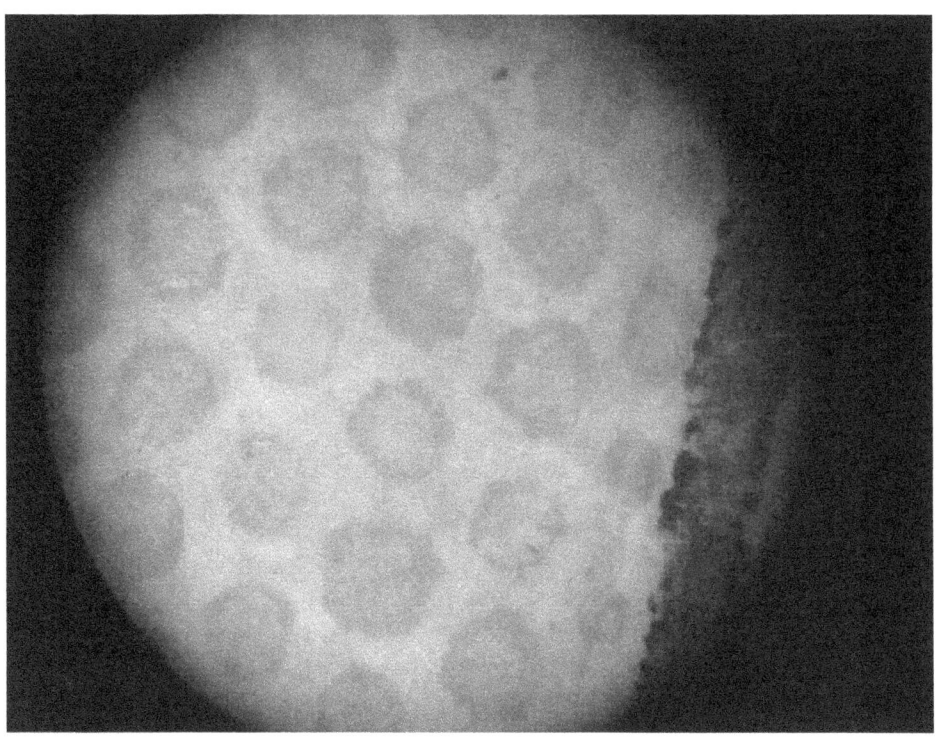

Circa 1910 chromolithograph. You won't mistake this for a 1980s Topps. It looks very similar to the color lithography on an 1880s baseball card

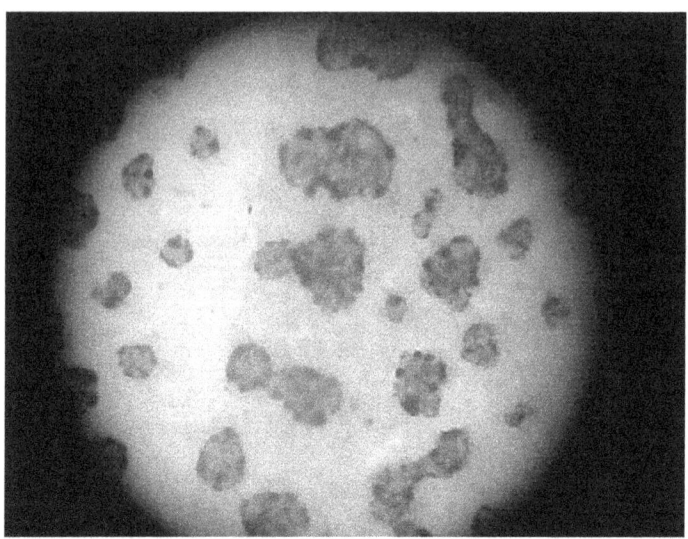

1910: These black half-tone dots are hardly uniform and some have the irregular rim.

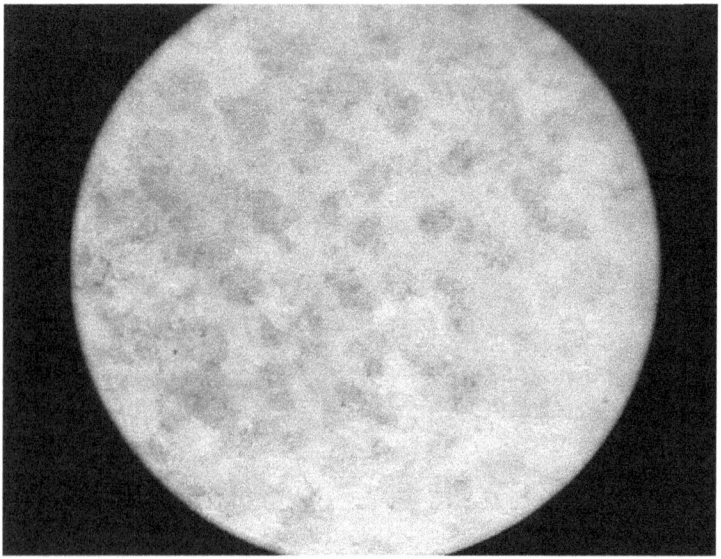

A different part on the same 1910 card. This could easily be mistaken for a Victorian lithograph.

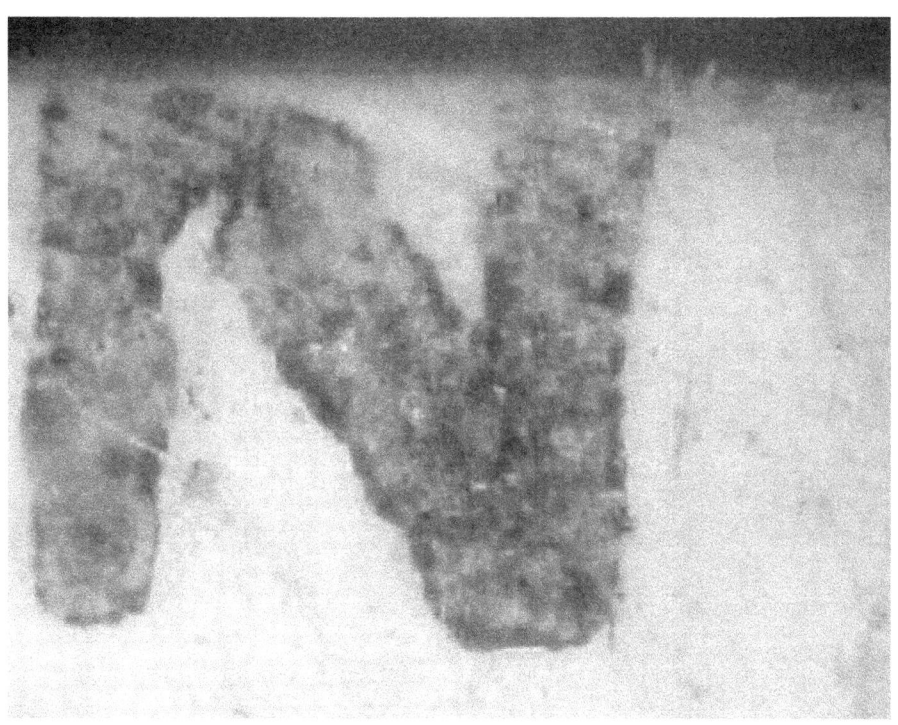

Typeset lettering on front of a T206. Notice the dark rim around the letter. This type of rim is a sure sign that the card is vintage.

## ( 16 )
## Another early printing method: photoengraving

A large number of early 1900s baseball cards were made with the photoengraving printing process. Photoengraving is an obsolete method that has not been used commercially for many years. This means that if you can identify that a card is a photoengraving, you can be assured it is old.

Photoengraving was used to make most of those early black and white cards with photo-realistic images of the players. Popular photoengraving issues include 1893 Just So Tobacco, 1915 Sporting News, vintage Exhibit cards, Fro Joy Babe Ruth, 1913 National Game, Fan Craze and 1923 Maple Crispette. A few photoengraving cards, most notably the 1914 and 1915 Cracker Jacks, have black and white pictures with one or two extra colors printed over (tinted).

An early 1900s baseball card with a photo-realistic image is either a photoengraving or 'real photo' (see next chapter).

Photoengraving is identified with a microscope. The photorealistic picture of the player will be made up of black and white half tone dots (the border, other text and designs will often be solid ink). This dot pattern is distinctly different from modern lithographed half tone dots. In areas, the pattern will resemble a waffle. The ink will have a distinct dark, mechanical rim or edge. This gives the printing an almost 3-D appearance. This rim was caused by the pressure of the printing plate during printing. The pressure pushed the excess ink to the edge. Some isolated dots will often have little crosses in the middle.

This dark rim appears not just with the half-tone dots but on any border lines, solid designs and text on the front of the card. If you look at Babe Ruth's name at the bottom of a 1915 Sporting News, you will see the dark rim around much to all of the lettering.

There are somewhat similar dark ink rims that appear on other early types of printing. This includes early chromolithography and woodcuts. Luckily, all of these types of 'rim' prints are also vintage. The presence of a microscopic rim is always a good sign authenticity-wise.

On many types of paper or cardstock, this rim is easily seen. On coarser paper, like newsprint or on the typical rough back of some cards, it is more difficult.

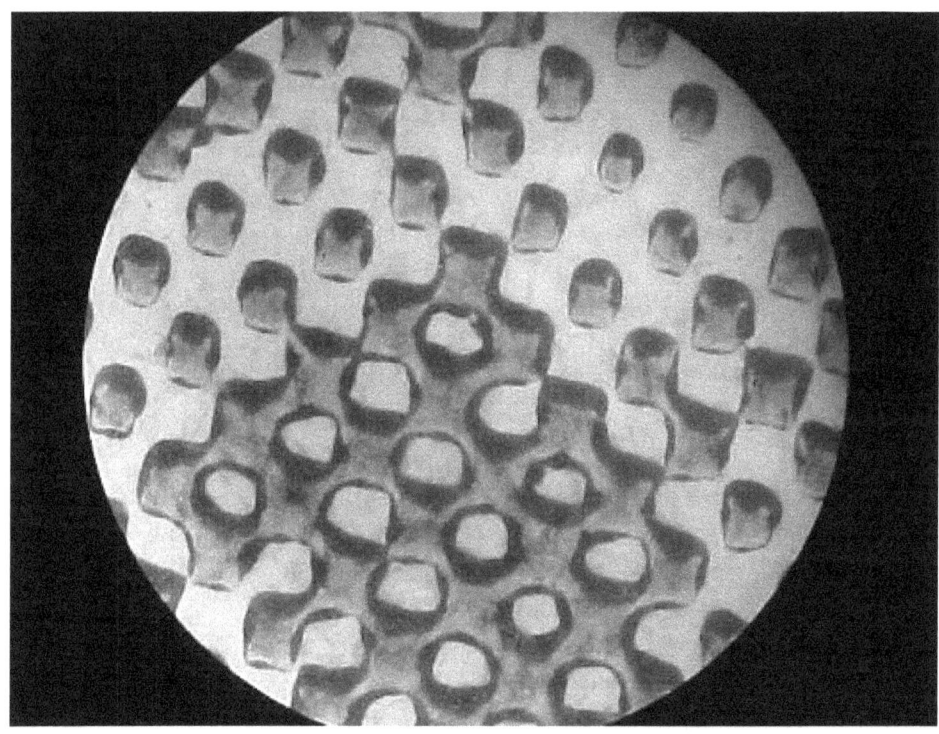

**Photoengraving:** The halftone dots have a distinct dark rim that gives the printing an almost 3D appearance. Notice that the isolated dots have little crosses in the middle. The dark rim and unique dot pattern proves that this printing is old. Compare this picture to the modern halftone pictures in chapter 12.

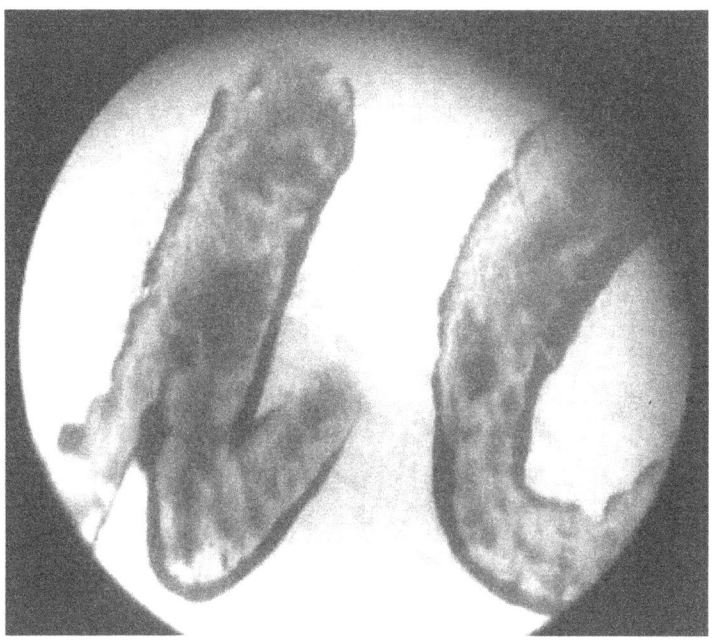

The lettering on this early photoengraving has a dark rim.

## (17)
## 'Real photo' baseball cards

T200 Fatima Team card

Many early baseball cards are not printing press and ink prints but actual photographs. These actual photograph cards are commonly referred to as 'real photo.' A majority of 1800s baseball cards are real photo. Though only a small number of 20$^{th}$ century cards are real photo, this includes a number of popular issues.

The following is a short list of real photo issues.

<u>1800s</u>: These are the cards with the sepia realistic images. N172 and N173 Old Judges, Gypsy Queen, SF Hess, Peck & Snider CDVs and trade cards, Four Base Hits, the Kalamazoo Bats issues, G & B Gum, Yum Yum Tobacco, Newsboy Cabinets. (Though they resemble real photo cards, with realistic images, the 1890s Just So and N300 Mayo are not real photo.)

<u>1900s</u>: T200 Fatima Team, Fatima Premium, T222 Fatima,

T5 Pinkerton Cabinet Cards.

**Distinguishing a photograph from a mechanical print: "Dots Versus No Dots"**
Not all realistic looking pictures are photographs, and the collector should be able to tell the difference between photographs and photomechanical prints (realistic pictures made by a printing press). The images in this book, for example, are not actual photographs but ink prints. The pictures in a newspaper or magazine or on most 20th century baseball cards are photomechanical reproductions of photographs.

While a mechanical print, like a lithograph or photoengraving, is made by a printing press pressing ink against paper or cardstock, a photograph is made by the subtle interaction of light with chemicals. A photographic image is made by a chemical process.

A handheld microscope, or even a strong magnifier, will allow one to easily distinguish between a photograph and a non-photograph. Close examination of a photograph will reveal great subtly in tones and shades. The tones can be so subtle that they seem as if you can't get the microscope into focus. Under the microscope, the photomechanical print will be made up of tiny dots or similar ink patterns.

**Most reprints of real photo cards have the halftone dot pattern**
The vast majority of reprints of known real photo cards are quickly identified due to the dot pattern in the player's image. If you see a dot pattern on an Old Judge or Four Base Hits, you know it's a reprint. A beginner with a strong magnifying glass should have no trouble identifying the average Old Judge or Fatima reprint.

As counterfeits and reprints occasionally (though rarely)

exist in real photo form, the following is a more in depth look at the processes used to make early real photo cards.

\* \* \* \*

**1800s real photo baseball cards : albumen prints**

1800s real photo baseball cards were made with the albumen photographic processes. They are often called albumen photographs or albumen prints. In photography, a photographic image on a piece of paper is commonly called a print, even though it wasn't made with a printing press.

While there were other types of photographs in the 1800s, the albumen print was by far the most common form of paper photograph in the United States and around the world. Nearly all 1860s-90s photographs, baseball cards or otherwise, are albumen. Even non-collectors associate horse-and-buggy pictures with the soft, sentimental tones that were produced by the albumen process.

Except for modernized versions made by a few advanced art photographers, the albumen process is as obsolete as the Model T. It hasn't been used commercially for about a century, having long ago been replaced by more advanced technology.

During its 19th century heyday, the albumen process was used by a wide range of photographers and for a wide range of photos. It was used by famous photographers and unknown small town studios. It was used to make the priceless photo hung today in a Paris or New York museum and the Joseph Hall cabinet card sold by Mastro Auctions, official portraits of Queen Victoria and many of the photos in your family collection. This means that, by studying the cabinet card of your great great uncle or that $2 cabinet you bought at a flea market, you are also studying the qualities of the Old Judge Cabinet.

The albumen process was time-consuming and difficult in the extreme compared to modern photography. Most practitioners were well-trained professionals with a working knowledge of chemistry. Except for a few technically gifted and wealthy hobbyists, there were no amateur photographers like today.

The process required a unique kind of chemically treated paper that was mostly imported from France and Germany. Photography is a chemical process and the photographer couldn't use any old typing or writing paper he got at the local dime store. Only a few factories in the world made albumen paper. This is lucky for us today, because this albumen paper has distinct qualities that are usually straightforward to identify.

One of the distinct qualities of 1800s albumen prints is that they are on super thin paper. The paper was so thin and delicate that the prints had to be mounted. This means that the photographic print was pasted to a heavy backing. Usually the backing is a sheet of cardboard, but albumen prints can also be found mounted in or on books, programs and other items. All 1800s albumen baseball cards have a cardboard backing. With the N172 Old Judges, the albumen print is the same size as the backing. With the N173 Old Judge and other cabinets cards the print is pasted to a larger backing.

The albumen images are usually well aged. This includes the common sepia or yellowish tone, often along with fading of the image details in areas and foxing (brownish redish age spots). Particularly due to different storage, the severity and type of aging will vary. For collectors, albumen photos are best stored away from light, excessive heat and humidity. An example of excessive heat is storing them next to a radiator. When originally made, albumen images were not sepia but closer to black and white. You will sometimes find examples that were well stored and retain these colors. Albumen images are often glossy.

Many albumen images have very fine web-like pattern of cracking. This is often seen up close with the naked eye. Sometimes a normal magnifying glass or loupe is needed. The cracking, which does not appear on all albumen prints, can be throughout the entire image or in isolated areas.

One of the keys to authenticating albumen prints is examining the image area under a microscope. Unlike with the later gelatin silver prints or Kodak photos, the paper fibers can be seen on the albumen print. It takes some practice, but with experience it's not difficult to see the paper fibers with a microscope of 50 or more power. When judging the authenticity of an expensive albumen photograph, for myself or others, I always take my trusty microscope and look for paper fibers in the image.

Though uncommon, it is possible to find 1880s albumen prints that are pink (by far the most common), blue, green, yellow and other bright colors. The process to add dye to the albumen paper was invented at this time. The pink old judges are commonly underdeveloped (too light).

Some albumen prints have a distinct effect called 'silvering.' Silvering is when it appears as if the silver has come to surface of the image. Sort of like a silver patina. If it exists, it is more noticeable in the dark areas of the image, and when viewed at a specific angle to the light. If you change the angle of the photo to a light source, the silvering will be come stronger and darker, sometimes disappearing. It can range in intensity. Sometimes it is only revealed under close examination when holding the photo nearing a 180 degree to a light. Sometimes it is obvious in an online auction image. Importantly for collectors, silvering is an aging process. In simple words, a photograph with natural silvering wasn't made recently.

100X view of an albumen print clearly showing the paper fibers. The presence of paper fibers in the player image is one of the surest signs of authenticity on a 1800s real photo card

## 1900s Real Photo Baseball Cards : Gelatin Silver

1914 Pinkerton Cabinet Card of Shoeless Joe Jackson, with a gelatin silver print affixed to a larger cardboard mount

Early 1900s real photo baseball cards were gelatin silver photographs, commonly called gelatin silver prints.

What albumen prints were to $19^{th}$ century photographs, gelatin silver prints were to early $20^{th}$ century photographs. Gelatin silver was by far the most common form of black and white photograph from the late 1890s to recent years. If you own a T200 Fatima team card, a 1930s movie still photo or a 1960s wirephoto, you own a gelatin silver photograph. If you go to an exhibit of original photographs by famous early $20^{th}$ century photographers, many to most will likely be gelatin silver prints. Those 1940s black and white snapshots in your family albums are more than likely gelatin silver.

While gelatin silver photographs were commonly used for many years, early examples have distinct qualities that help the collector to identify them as vintage.

Many gelatin silver photographs have stark black and white images, distinct to the sepia tones of an albumen print. However, many vintage gelatin silver images are found with sepia tones, sometimes closely resembling 1800s albumen prints. This sepia tinge is most often caused by the toning of the paper, but was sometimes intentionally created by the photographer.

Though not as thin as albumen paper, early gelatin silver paper is thin. The earlier the thinner. The modern 'double weight' photo paper was not popularly introduced until after the scope of this guide. An example of double weight paper is the typical modern autographed 8x10 photo.

Most vintage gelatin silver paper (as seen on the back of the photo) will be off white and often with toning and foxing. Counter to intuition, however, the earliest examples, say 1902 or 1904, typically has bright white paper, though still with occasional foxing, soiling and other discoloration. The earliest paper was handmade without wood pulp. Wood pulp, introduced to later photo paper production, is what makes later photos and newspapers turn brown. The earliest handmade gelatin silver paper was naturally white and, since there was no wood pulp, did not tone with age. This means that you should not be distressed if the paper on your 1903 Honus Wagner photo is so much brighter than on your 1920s photo cards.

Many early gelatin silver prints are mounted in similar fashion to albumen prints. Most are unmounted (plain paper photograph with no cardboard backing). The T5 Pinkerton Cabinets are mounted just like an N173 Old Judge or Newsboy Cabinet. The T200 and T222 are just a photographic print on thin paper with no cardboard backing.

Unlike albumen prints, the paper fibers in the gelatin silver print cannot be seen under a microscope. The gelatin silver photos have a thin layer of gelatin on the image surface. The gelatin was used to hold the needed photographic chemicals to the paper. While transparent, the gelatin obscures the paper fibers from view. When viewing under a microscope, you may see the uneven surface of the gelatin. With experience this surface is easily distinguished from paper fibers.

**Silvering as the best sign of authenticity**
Many, though not all, early 1900s real photo cards have some degree of silvering. Silvering is less likely to appear on photos with underexposed images. Genuine silvering is one of the surest signs of authenticity. If that $5,000 Fatima Premium that you just bought has silvering, and otherwise looks the way a Fatima Premium should, you can be confident that your purchase is authentic.

### Ray-O-Prints and Other Self-Developing Photos

Ray O Print of Babe Rut

Around 1930 M.P.& Co issued several photo-kit issues for kids. The best known set was the Ray-O-Print kit that included of Babe Ruth, Lou Gehrig, Mary Pickford, Herbert Hoover, and other celebrities. Each kit consisted of an envelope containing a photographic negative of one celebrity and a piece of photographic paper about the size of a trading card. This allowed a kid to make one photo card.

It is possible in modern times to make multiple copies of from the original negative by getting more photo paper. It is safest for the collector to buy a Ray-O-Print photograph when it is accompanied by the original kit. This not only makes authenticity sense, but the accompanying kit raises the value and desirability of the photo card. The entire kit with photo is not often seen on the market.

Black light tests will identify most modern photographic paper. The presence of silvering will prove that a photo card is old, even when there is no accompanying kit. Particularly thin photo paper will also be evidence of old age.

There were other Pre-WWII self developing photo cards. Again, the presence of silvering will assure the collector that the card is genuine, even if there is no kit. Most of the non Ray O Print issues are scarce to very rare, and reprinting from the original negatives is not known to be a problem. In some cases, a negative for a card may no longer exist, even if an example of the card is known.

Circa 1920 gelatin silver photograph with strong silvering in the black areas. Silvering often resembles a silver patina.

## (18)
## Final note on printing

The previous chapters covered the mechanical and photographic printing methods used to make the majority of standard trading cards. This does not mean that the collector will not find genuine cards that do not fit neatly into the previous descriptions and pictures. Some European cards and obscure 1800s American trade cards were made with out of the ordinary printing methods. If the standard card printing is on rough card or paper stock, it may be difficult to make a perfect opinion about the printing. If you look at non-card items, like postcards, premium prints or advertising posters, you should expect to find unusual printing techniques. There are one or two early color baseball premiums and notebook covers that used an early form of halftone color lithography and have a primitive form of color halftone dots. For these non-card items and obscure areas outside your experience, dealing with reputable sellers and getting second opinions, including that of your trusted grader, is important.

Luckily, even if you are unfamiliar with etching, engraving or other lesser used techniques, you can still identify many modern reprints with your black light.

## ( 19 )
## Altered counterfeits

Some baseball card counterfeits are otherwise genuine cards that have been doctored. This usually involves making a slight alteration in order to transform a common card into a rare and expensive variation. Famous variations include the T206 Magie error (misspells the last name of Sherry Magee), T206 Doyle variation and the 1990 Topps NNOF (No Name on Front) Frank Thomas rookie card.

The collector should take extra care when purchasing expensive variations. This can include getting second opinions, whether from a fellow collector or trusted grader, and purchasing from a good seller.

Altered counterfeits is an area where you can get a worthwhile opinion from a non collector. While you may be the resident baseball card guru, your spouse or daughter may turn out to have a keener eye for seeing alterations.

**Methods for identifying altered cards**
A combination of the following tests will identify most altered counterfeits

**Visual Examination**: Added paper and paint is often identified just by a close look. It is often a slightly off color, pattern and/or texture. It is difficult to match colors to fool the human eye. While most amateurs can be easily detected, some professional restoration can be deceptive.

**Surface Texture:** When holding a card at an angle nearing 180 degrees to a light, the added paint, ink or paper will often have a different texture and gloss from the rest of the surface. The added material also may be physically raised from the rest of the card. You might be able to feel the relief with your finger tip.

It is extremely difficult to match the gloss of the original, and chances are added paper or ink will shine differently.

The added paint on this fake 1990 Topps NNOF Frank Thomas is obvious when viewed at a sharp angle to the desk lamp. The paint has a different gloss and texture.

**Opacity**: When held up to a bright light, the doctoring may be apparent.

**Black Light:** Added paper, glue and ink often fluoresces differently under black light.

**Beware of 'varnished' counterfeits**
To try and cover up their handiwork, some forgers will coat the card in a clear substance. This often makes the touchups harder to see with the naked eye. However, the varnish will usually give the card an abnormal gloss and florescence. Comparison with genuine cards in the same issue will reveal the difference.

A collector bought a rare variation T206 card. The card looked okay to him, except the front was much glossier than his other T206s. The card turned out to be an altered card that had been varnished.

# ( 20 )
## Provenance

Provenance is where something came from and who owned it, examined it or handled it along the way. When we hear the word we often think of the sale of a millions dollar Modigliani painting or George Custer's military uniform and not baseball cards. However, good provenance is relevant to judging the authenticity of a card.

Good provenance includes that a rare card was verifiably sold by a respected dealer or auction house or was otherwise judged authentic by someone knowledgeable. A card that is entombed and graded by a top grader is an example of good provenance. The label above the card documents that card was examined in person by the company.

Top graders and sellers make mistakes like everyone else, so provenance in and of itself does not prove authenticity. However, if a good dealer believes the card is authentic and you, as expert collector, agree, the card is more than likely authentic. "The card looks good to me plus I bought it from a reputable seller" is always a good combination. Good provenance can be considered the equivalent of a good second opinion.

The more expensive and the less your familiarity with a card, the more important the provenance.

Many sellers of counterfeits make up histories for the cards, just as many forgers make up histories for Babe Ruth autographed balls the forged last week. One reason I try to buy from honest people is because they're honest. If a seller you know to be honest says he got baseball signed in person by Willie Mays, that's because he got the ball signed in person by Willie Mays. And if he says the Hollywood poster came from Sotheby's auction lot #882, you know the poster came from Sotheby's lot #882.

## (21)
## Assorted Notes

Beware of eBay sellers who use only funky photos of expensive cards. This includes photos out of focus, several photos none which show the entire card, bizarre angles and overly distracting, even psychedelic backgrounds. There often is a reason the seller doesn't want you to have a clear look at the card.

\* \* \* \*

**Paper stock cutouts**
A few unscrupulous sellers on eBay sell paper pictures cut out from old publications, offering them as baseball cards. These cutouts have little to no long term value. They often have partial articles or ads on back, making it obvious that they are not whole cards.
  It is not hard for even the beginner to avoid these non-cards. These sellers often use private eBay auctions, and the cards are in the holders of dubious graders. Reputable graders like PSA and SGC do not grade these scraps. A beginner who sticks to cards listed in the Standard Catalog of Baseball Cards will automatically skip these cutouts as they are not listed.

\* \* \* \*

Scammers sometimes offer scans of real cards that they

don't own. This is often of high end high graded cards, the images stolen from a Mastro Auction or similar. When making a thousands dollar purchase, you want to be confident of the seller's reliability, not just that the card in the picture looks okay.

\* \* \* \*

If a deal looks too good to be true, it usually is. You can't get a PSA9 1952 Mickey Mantle for 1/5th the normal price and no one's going to give you T206 Honus Wagner for $2,000. They might give you a reprint for $2,000 but not an original.

\* \* \* \*

If a seller is offering a rare baseball card with obviously scissors clipped corners that he describes as having "natural corner wear," there's a more than probable chance you're looking at a fake.

With homemade fakes, one of the harder things to do is to mimic natural corner rounding, The forger often clips the corners at a straight angle then roughs them up a bit. In many cases, the corners remain obviously hand cut.

Of course genuine cards can have clipped corners, but anyone experienced with cards can tell the difference between clipping and natural wear. Even if there is the odd chance the card for sale is real, why would you choose to make expensive purchases from a seller who can't identify obvious trimming? Shouldn't you be buying from the seller who can tell the difference?

\* \* \* \*

1913 National Game and other cards have rounded corners

that were professionally cut and are uniform throughout the entire issue. Many cheap counterfeits are easy to identify in an online auction, as the corners are not cut evenly, are different corner to corner and/or are different compared to the corners on real cards. Simply comparing the corners to a picture of a known genuine card will weed out most reprints and fakes.

\* \* \* \*

Unless they really know what they are doing, collectors should only purchase T206 Honus Wagner, T206 Ed Plank, and similar big time cards from top sellers and/or with the help of a trusted card expert.

Buy a T206 Wagner from a stranger at your own risk.

\* \* \* \*

Many home computer counterfeits will reproduce the dirt on the original card. Even the 'dirt' on that fake T206's white border is made up of the multi-color dot pattern.

\* \* \* \*

The T5 Pinkerton cabinets have real photographs (gelatin silver prints) pasted to the cardboard backing. The related 1910s 'Pinkerton Postcards' are photoengravings that can have blank backs or generic scorecards printed on back. You will occasionally find one of the blank backs that has been used as a postcard, with handwritten address and note, stamp and 1910s postmark. Sometimes the T5 photographic prints can be found without the cardboard mount.

On genuine T5s, the paper photos were sometimes affixed loosely and crookedly.

\* \* \* \*

Many 1800s cards, trade cards and scraps were originally pasted into albums. The vintage glue that can still be on the back of the cards is typically light brown and thin, distinct to modern Elmer's glue.

\* \* \* \*

Most sport and non-sport 1800s trade cards were on a thin stock, like a stiff paper.

\* \* \* \*

Some T206 reprints have obviously oversized borders and/or different text font on front.

\* \* \* \*

W517s with "W517" printed on the bottom border are reprints. Some people trim the bottom to remove this text.

\* \* \* \*

**Observe what genuine toning and wear looks like.**
Genuine toning is even and throughout the card. It doesn't look like someone painted it on or the card was dipped in a cup of strong tea.
    Many fakes were apparently cooked in the oven to make the card look toned and old. These baked cards often have an unreal darkness around the edge that does not resemble genuine toning. They look liked oven baked cooies.

\* \* \* \*

The 1914-15 Cracker Jacks cards have no white ink. The white on the cards is created by the absence of ink on the light colored cardstock. In other words, the white borders is the color of cardstock surface. If the Cracker Jack player picture has a large white section of his uniform that directly touches the boarder, there should be little or no difference in tone between the border white and the white of the uniform. On many reprint, there is a distinct difference between border and white uniform.

In a similar vein, most baseball cards used no white ink. So the comparison of the whiteness of the white border to the whiteness in the image can be important.

Original Cracker Jack HonusWagner. See how the white of his uniform naturally blends into the white of the border. In areas it's impossible to pinpoint where the uniform ends and the border begins.

\* \* \* \*

There are cases where genuine T206 cards have had rare backs artificially pasted to the back. The strange edges of the card often give it away.

\* \* \* \*

**Most proofs aren't proofs**
The baseball hobby puts a premium in price on card proofs. Proofs were pre-production test cards used to check graphics and text before the final printing. Early proofs are often blank backed, sometimes on different stock, with hand cut borders and little crosses on the borders. The crosses where used to line up the colors during the printing.

There are vintage items on the market that resemble proofs but are not. Many blank back 'cards' were cut from vintage notebooks, posters and signs. As they are hand cut and have blank backs, they are often marketed as proofs. These cutouts are less valuable than proofs.

One occasionally finds 'printer's scraps' that are sometimes misidentified as proofs. These scraps were from a printer's rejected sheet, often with poorly printed images, bad color registration and other graphics problems-- which is why the sheet was rejected. These reject sheets were rescued from the trash bin, and the single cards hand cut off. The cuts are usually funky, sometimes oversized. Many of those freakish prints (ghost prints, psychedelic color and major registration problems) were printer's scraps.

If you aren't sure if that blank back card in auction is a proof, it's safest to assume it isn't. The majority of blank back cards are not.

\* \* \* \*

**1880s album cutout cards**

In the 1880s, tobacco companies issued premium albums that pictured their popular trading cards. The cards look like real trading cards, except they are printed as part of the ornate album page. The albums are too valuable today for anyone to mess with, but in the old days a kid sometimes cut out the cards. One sees these cutout cards on the market. While an album cutout of Cap Anson or King Kelly has some financial value, it is worth only a fraction of the real card.

The cutouts are easily differentiated from the real cards. The cutouts have blank backs. Some cutout cards have overlapping designs from the album page. Buchner Gold Coin 'cards' cut from rare advertising posters have distinct overlapping text.

Though blank backed, N28 Allen & Ginters cutouts are the most often mistaken for regular cards as they have no overlapping designs. If cut too large, these cutouts often have dark edges unlike the real cards. The black was from the surrounding background on the album page.

\* \* \* \*

Many early paper premium and supplement baseball prints were photoengravings. This includes the Baseball Magazine premiums, Police Gazette Supplements and Sporting News Supplements.

\* \* \* \*

If you can identify photoengraving under the microscope, you can identify the original Fro Joy Babe Ruth baseball cards. Only the originals are photengravings. The reprints are lithographs and probably some home computer prints.

If you aren't confident that you can authenticate them, purchase from a very knowledgeable seller, have it checked out by someone knowledgeable or buy another Ruth issue. There are a lot more fake than real Fro Joy Ruths, so it best to play it safe with these cards.

\* \* \* \*

Since the dawn of scamming, it is a common scammer's technique to appear ignorant about what he is selling (often a fake he made himself!), and have the buyer believe he is getting a steal from this dim bulb of a seller. The scammer will say something on the order of:

> "This card looks real to me. But as I'm not an expert, I am calling it a reprint to be safe and offering it at a deep discount."

> "I found this Sweet Caporal Honus Wagner card. A local card shop says it looks like the real deal and is worth lots of money. But I don't know for sure so I'm offering it for $5,000."

The purchaser in these sales correctly believes there's a rube involved in the sale, but incorrectly believes it's the seller.

\* \* \* \*

**Old Judge Proofs**
There are both genuine and fake Old Judge Proofs on the market. The genuine proofs look just like the N173 Old Judge Cabinets (same size, shape, style mount, often with gilded edges), except the bottom panel has the name of a local studio instead of Old Judge Cigarettes. The albumen prints often have a Goodwin & Co. embossed stamp. The images for the Old Judges were shot by private studios in

various cities. This explains why the proofs have a local studio name on the bottom panel.

A series of later made 'proofs' that appear from time to time in auction do not have the same shape and style as the N173 Cabinets. Some are framed behind glass, with three photographic prints on one dark mount. Others come on unusually shaped cardboard mounts. Most of the fake mounts are dark. The photographic prints have a varnish-like covering which gives them an antique and cracked appearance. These fakes are real photo and have clear images. There's a good chance that they were made from the original Old Judge negatives which are known to exist. It has been speculated (perhaps correctly) that the proofs are old, perhaps from the early 1900s. Some consider them to have collector value due to this perceived age, though they are worth much less financially than the genuine proofs and Old Judge cabinets.

\* \* \* \*

Albumen prints can have some fluorescence under black light. So don't fret if your Old Judge or Newboy Cabinet has a bit of a glow.

\* \* \* \*

### Fake "Freeman Hans Wagner" Card with an interesting story

From time to time, one sees offered for sale the next page pictured Freeman Cigar Co. Card depicting Honus (Hans) Wagner. Though often sold as vintage, the card was made recently.

There are authentic early 1900s Hans Wagner tobacco labels, printed on white paper and to be stuck onto tobacco boxes. The labels are rare, and come in various designs. The most expensive examples will most likely be offered by major auction houses or top dealers. One of the labels has a close design to this card .... As a side note, in similar fashion to the T206 Wagner, this brand of tobacco was apparently never issued to the public. All the labels known to exist were never used.

**fake Honus Wagner card**

About 1993, a manufacture of collectable tin signs (you those Ted Williams Moxie and Joe Jackson H & B reprints) made a sign based on the design of just mentioned tobacco label. This man was selling them as modern collectables, not representing themselves as vintage. The sign was not an exact copy of the label. He added the 5 cents sign at the bottom for artistic balance. He also he used a different text font in parts as he could not find a modern duplicate.

A couple of years ago a man used a computer printer to reprint the tin signs as the tobacco trade cards-- naturally roughing and scuffing the cards to make them appear old. He sold them at flea markets to unsuspecting non-collectors who knew the legend of Honus Wagner and thought they had struck gold.

When shown a picture of one of the trade cards, the tin sign maker himself said it could not be genuine as it had his 1993 design.

David Rudd Cycleback is an art historian and science writer. His other books include *Judging the Authenticity of Photographs, Judging the Authenticity of Prints by the Masters, Ultraviolet Light and Black Light, Numeral Systems as Language: An introduction to ancient and modern numeration systems for the non-mathematician,* and *What's the Hair Color of Your Dream Lover? Why?: A look at how humans think and see.*

www.ingramcontent.com/pod-product-compliance
Lightning Source LLC
Chambersburg PA
CBHW021022090426
42738CB00007B/873